Alfred's Rudimental Duets

for Intermediate Snare Drummers

Jay Wanamaker

Jay Wanamaker is highly regarded as a percussion educator, arranger and clinician. He holds a B.M.E. degree from the Crane School of Music at Potsdam State University in New York and an M.M. degree in Percussion Performance from the University of Kansas. Jay has instructed many mass percussion sections for special events including the 1984 Summer Olympic Games, the rededication of the Statue of Liberty, the Pan American Games, Super Bowl XXII and the McDonald's All-American High School Band. He has served on the music faculty at the University of Southern California and has authored over 50 percussion publications.

Jay is currently on the Board of Directors of the Percussive Arts Society and serves as General Manager for the Yamaha Corporation of America in Buena Park, California.

Dedicated to my nephew, percussionist Chad Evans

CONTENTS

Bombastic	2
Rhythm in Motion	4
Corps Master	6
Ram & Jam	8
Chop Breaker	10
Drums on Parade	12
Colossus	14
Chop Builders	16

Copyright © MCMXCV by Alfred Publishing Co., Inc.
All rights reserved.   Printed in USA.

Book production
and music engraving:
Bruce Goldes

Bombastic

Jay Wanamaker

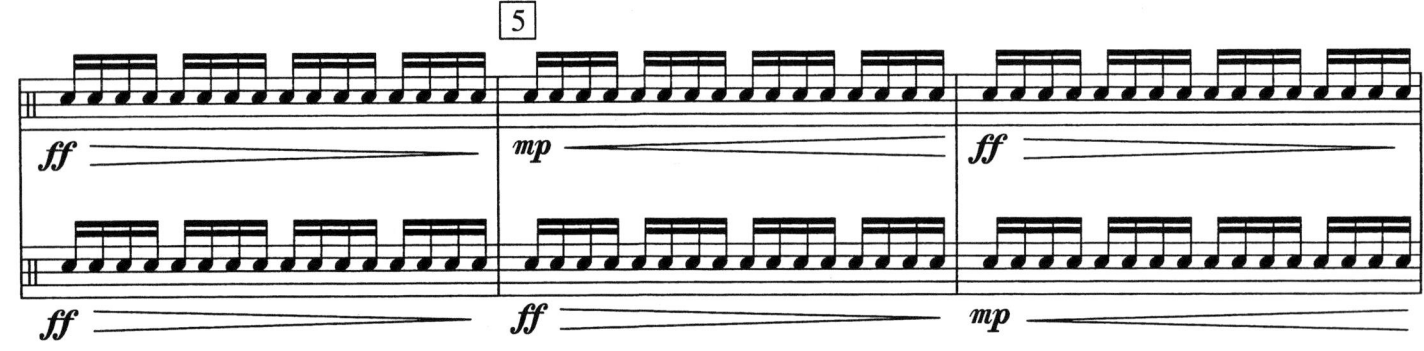

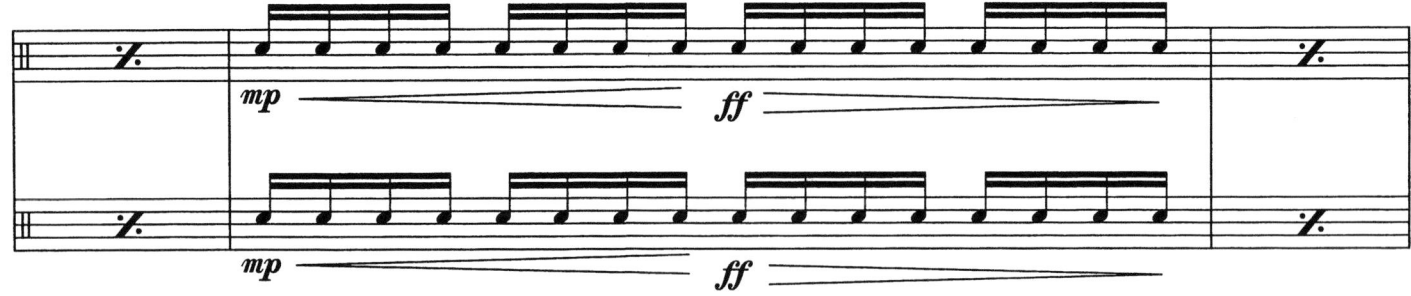
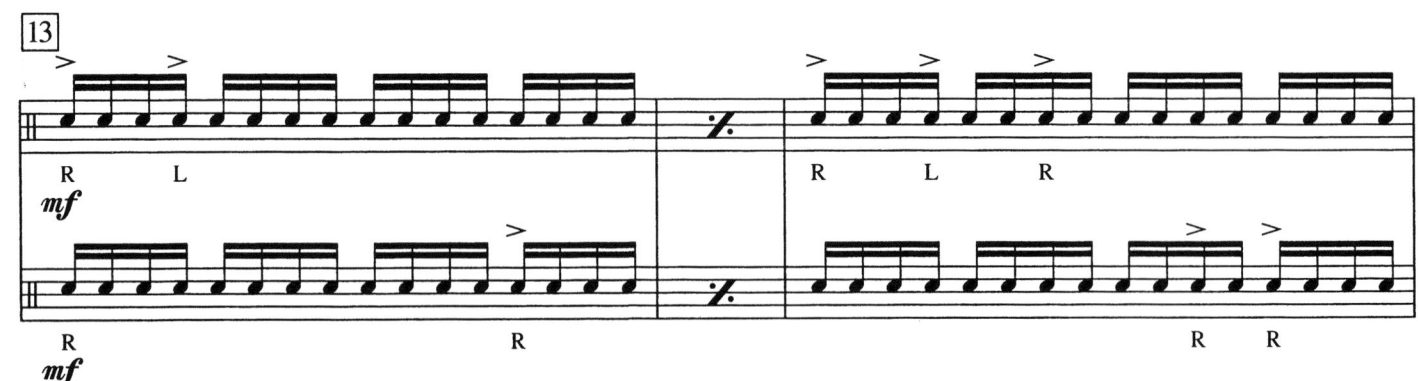

Copyright © MCMXCV by Alfred Publishing Co., Inc.
All rights reserved.   Printed in USA.

Legend:
R.S. (Rim Shot)   Strike the drum so that the stick strikes the drumhead and rim simultaneously.

Rhythm in Motion

Jay Wanamaker

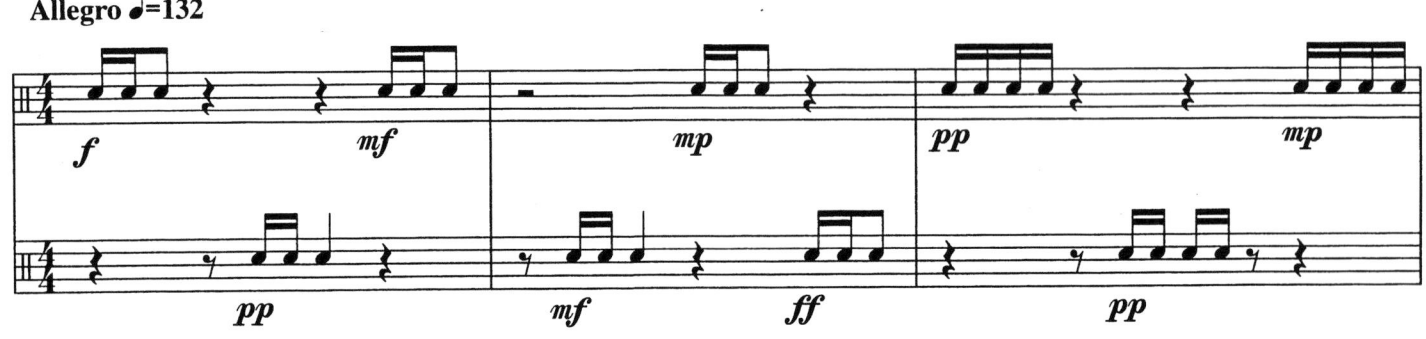
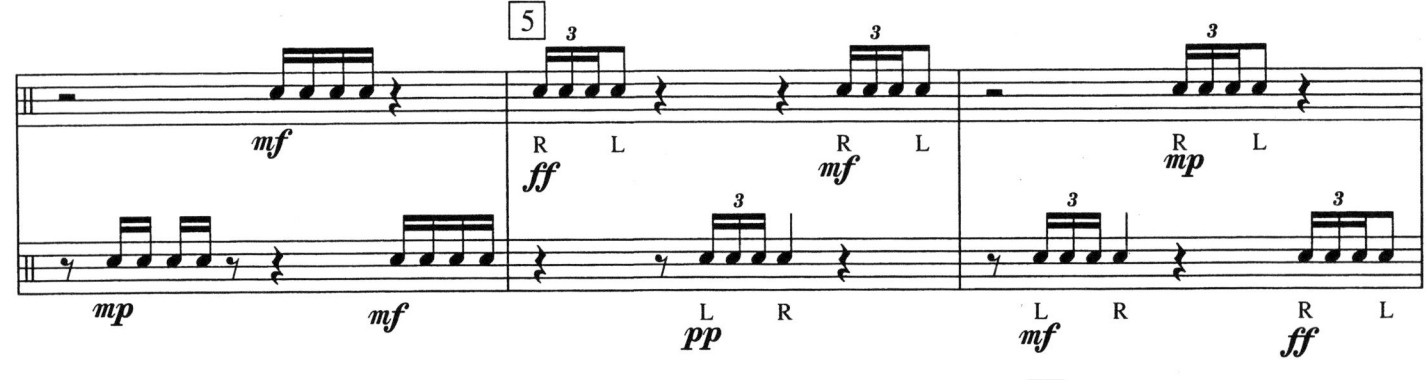
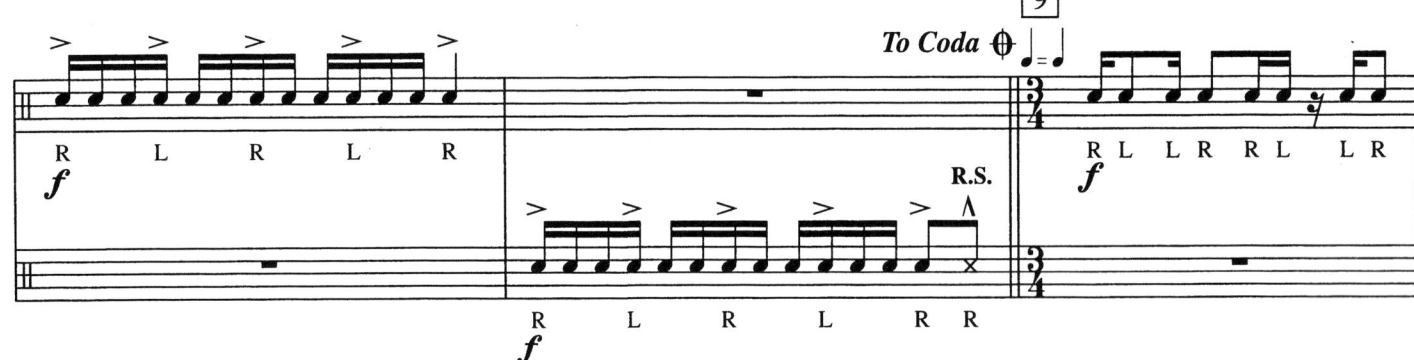
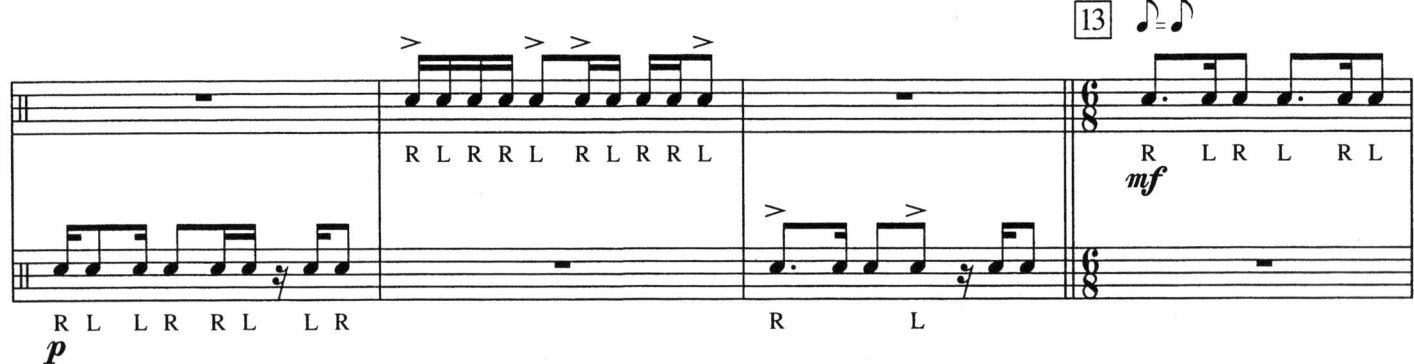
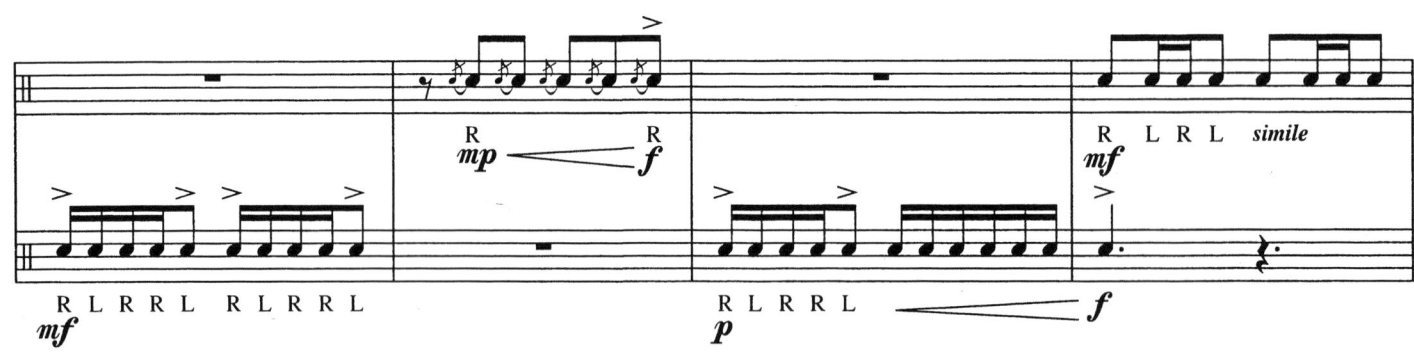

Copyright © MCMXCV by Alfred Publishing Co., Inc.
All rights reserved. Printed in USA.

Corps Master

Jay Wanamaker

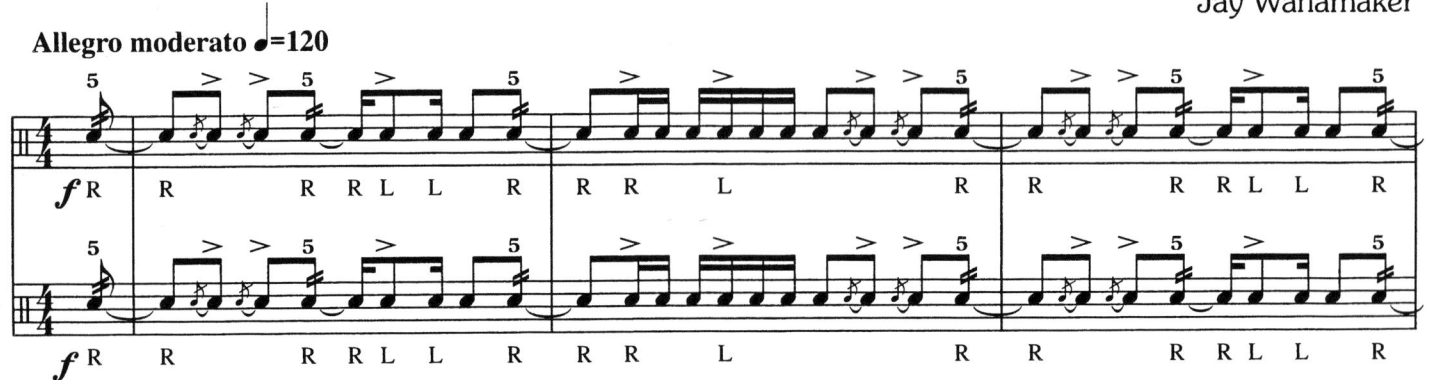

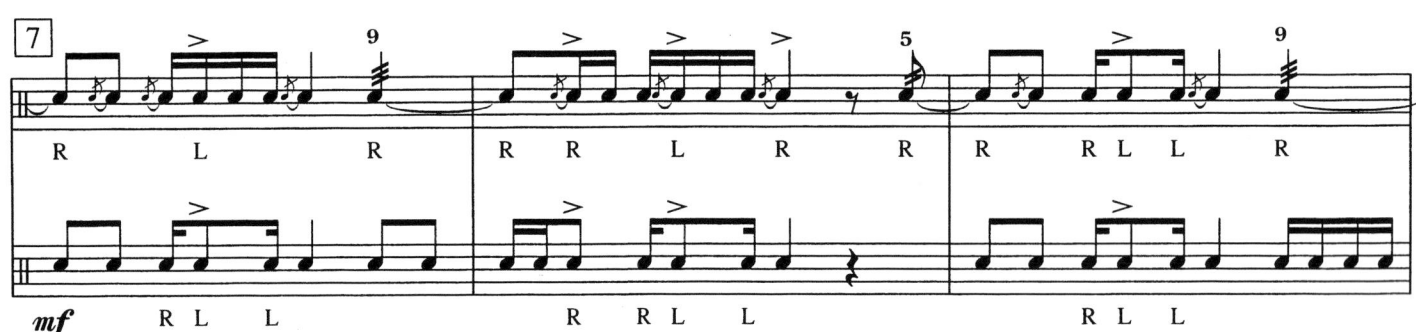

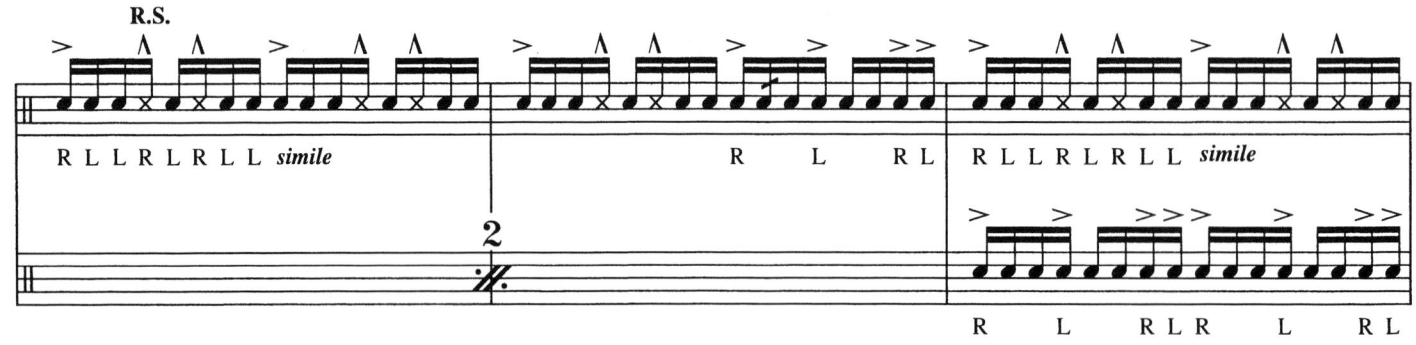

Copyright © MCMXCV by Alfred Publishing Co., Inc.
All rights reserved.   Printed in USA.

Legend:

S.S. (Stick Shot)   Strike the right stick on the left stick while the left stick is partway on the drum and rim.

R.S. (Rim Shot)   Strike the drum so that the stick strikes the drumhead and rim simultaneously.

Ram & Jam

Jay Wanamaker

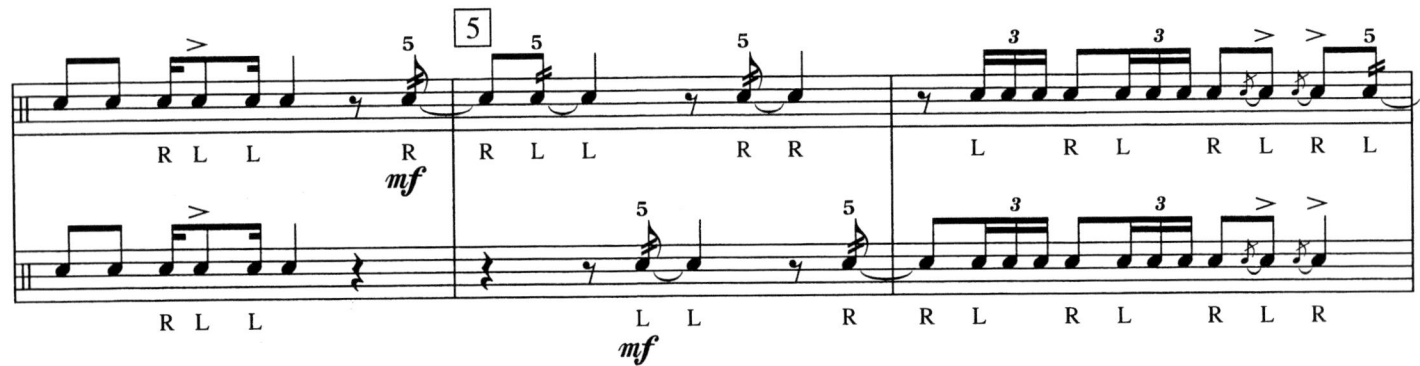
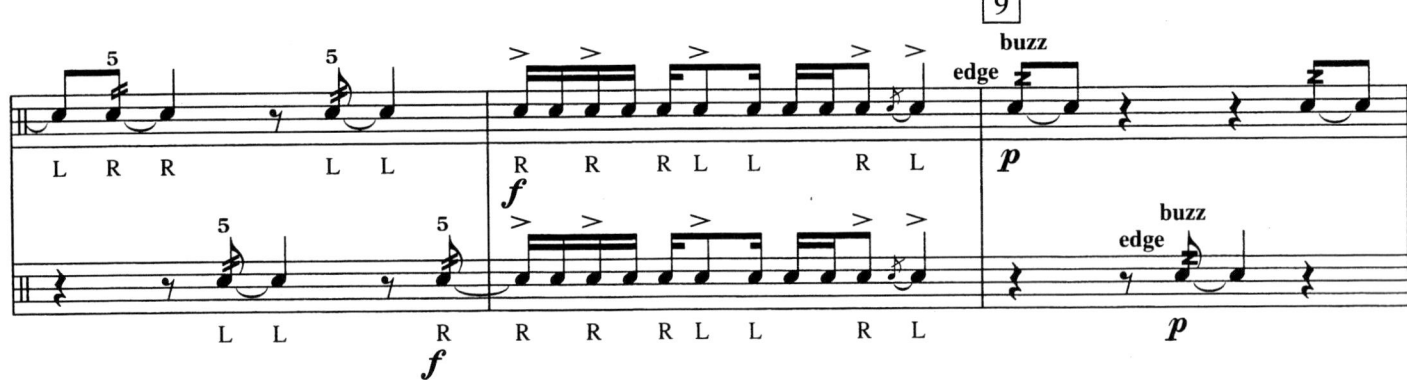

Copyright © MCMXCV by Alfred Publishing Co., Inc.
All rights reserved. Printed in USA.

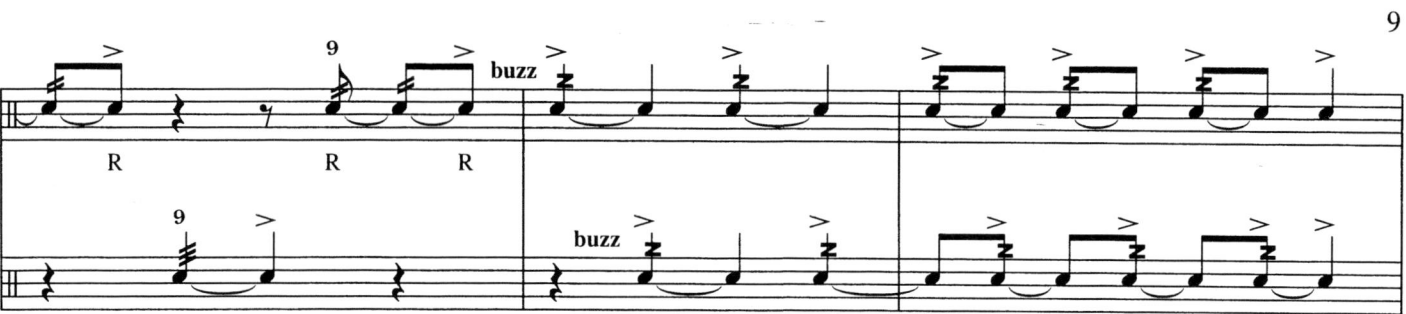

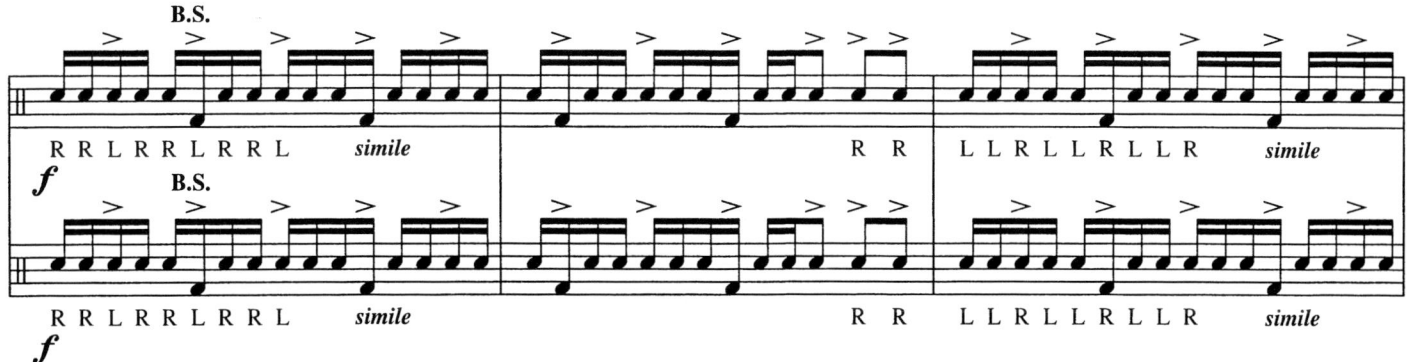

Legend:
R.S. (Rim Shot)   Strike the drum so that the stick strikes the drumhead and rim simultaneously.
B.S. (Back Stick)   Strike the drumhead with the butt ends of the drumsticks.

Chop Breaker

Jay Wanamaker

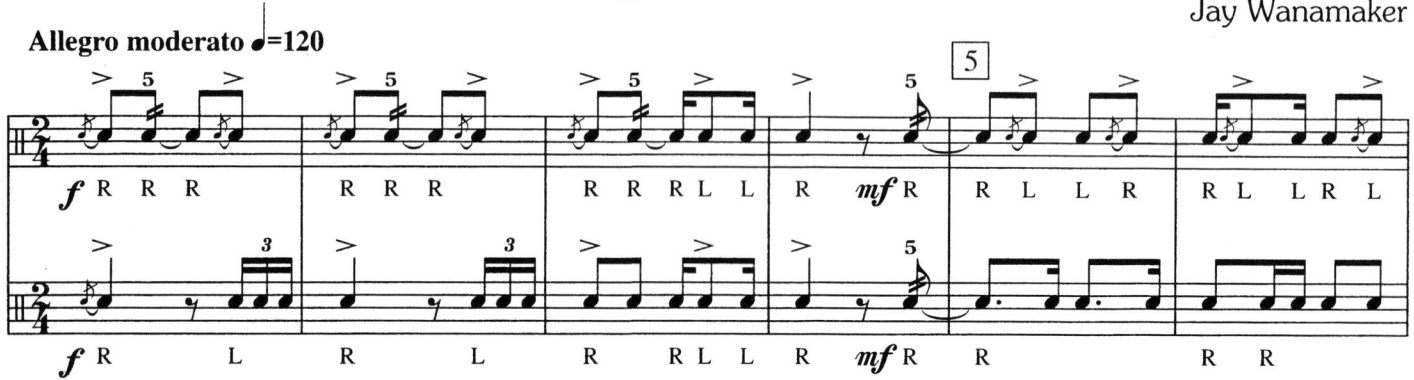
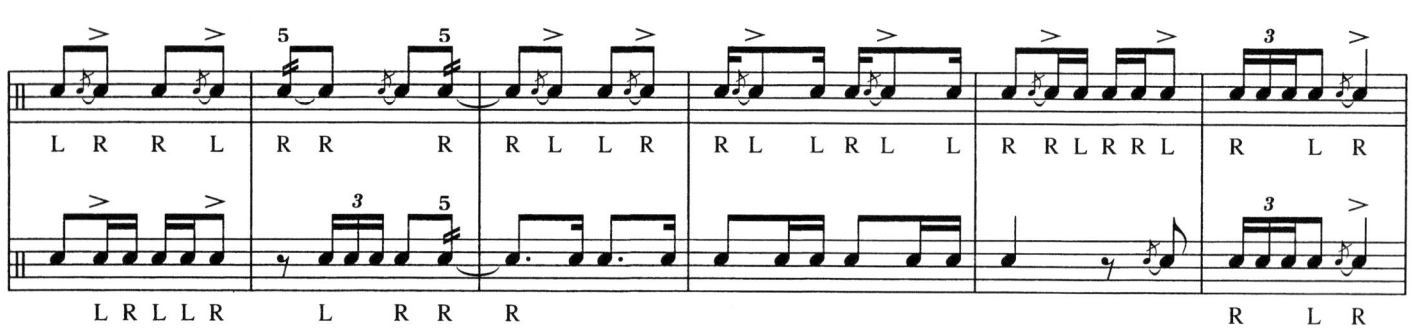
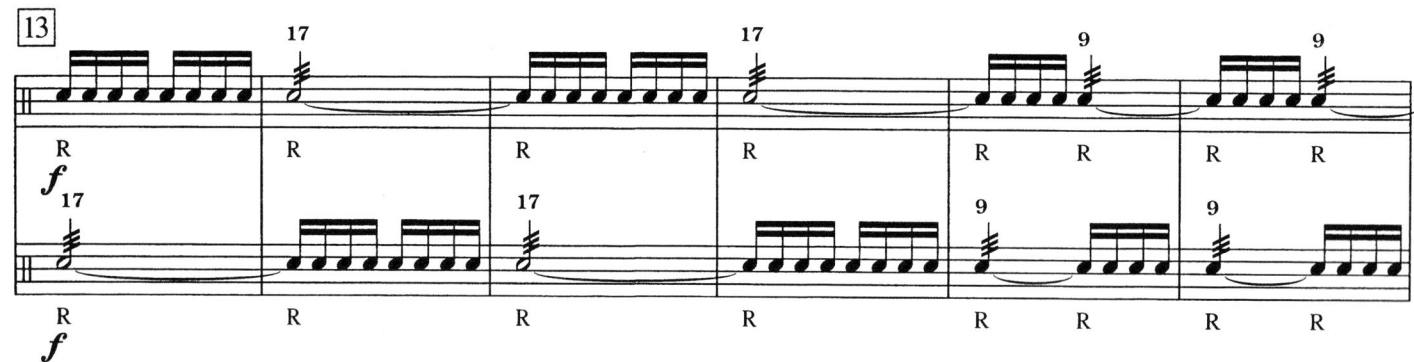

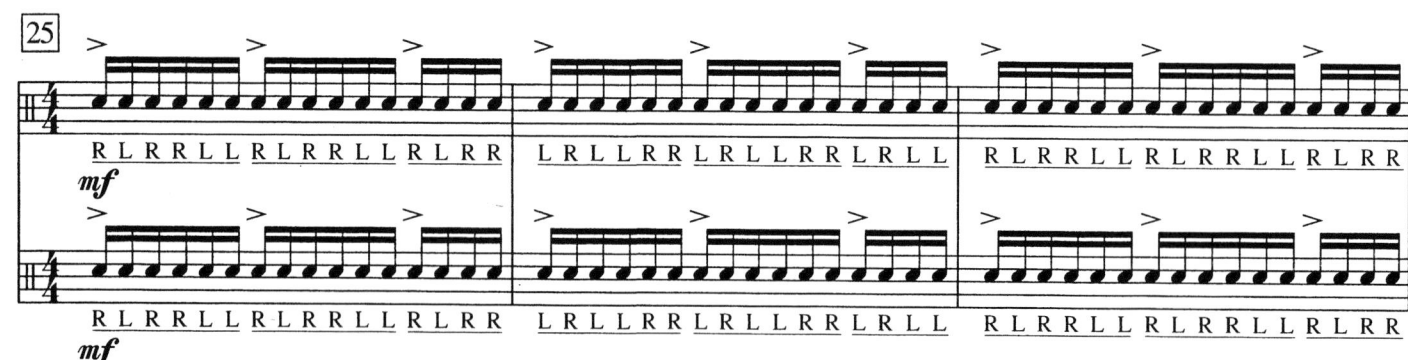

Copyright © MCMXCV by Alfred Publishing Co., Inc.
All rights reserved. Printed in USA.

Legend:
R.S. (Rim Shot)   Strike the drum so that the stick strikes the drumhead and rim simultaneously.

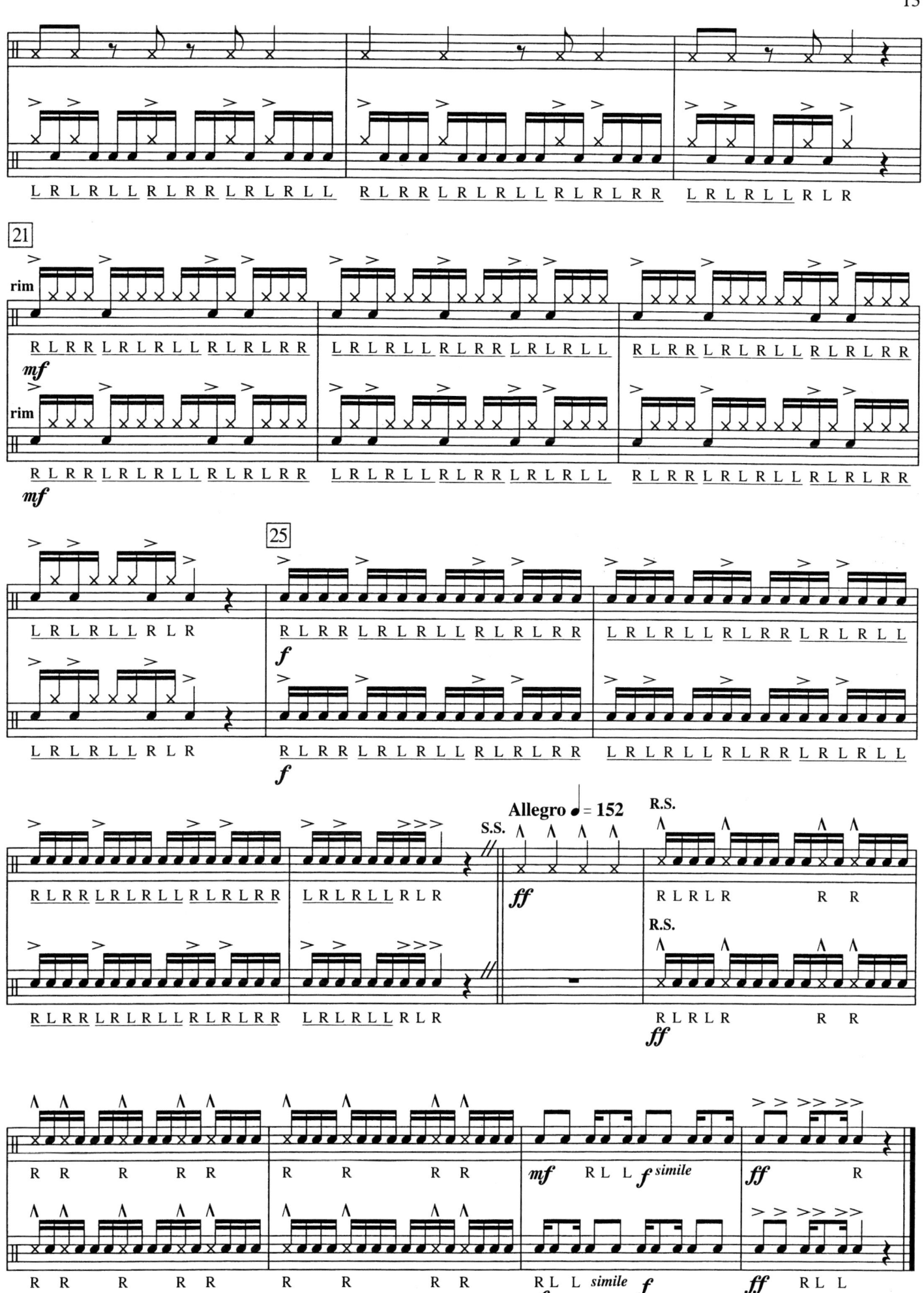

Colossus

Jay Wanamaker

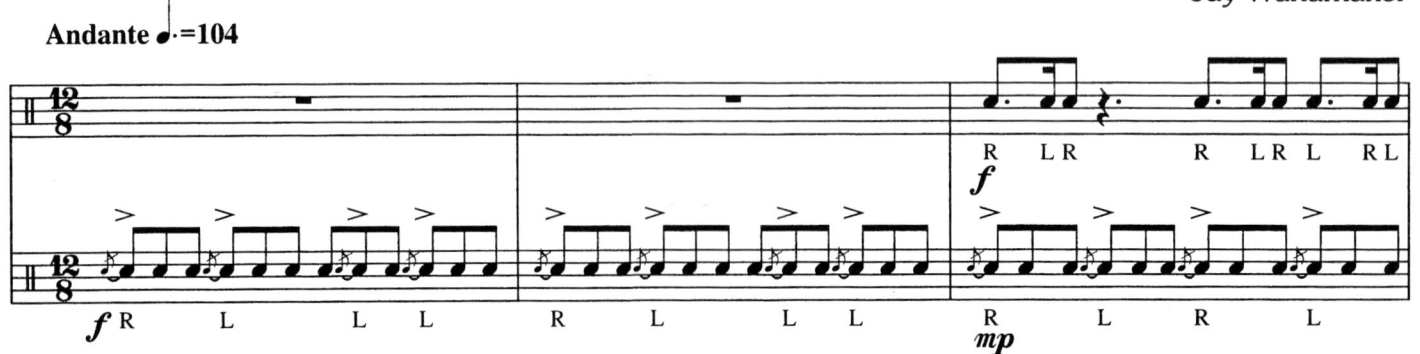

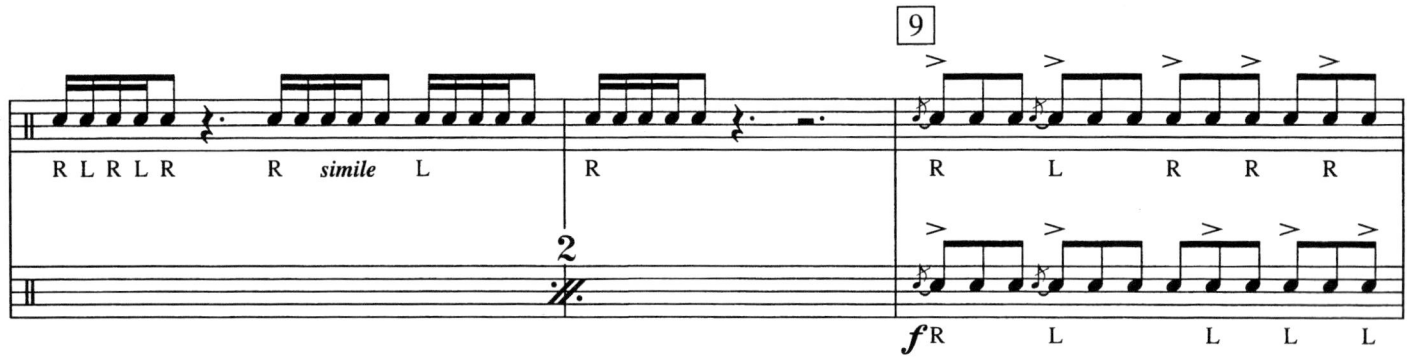
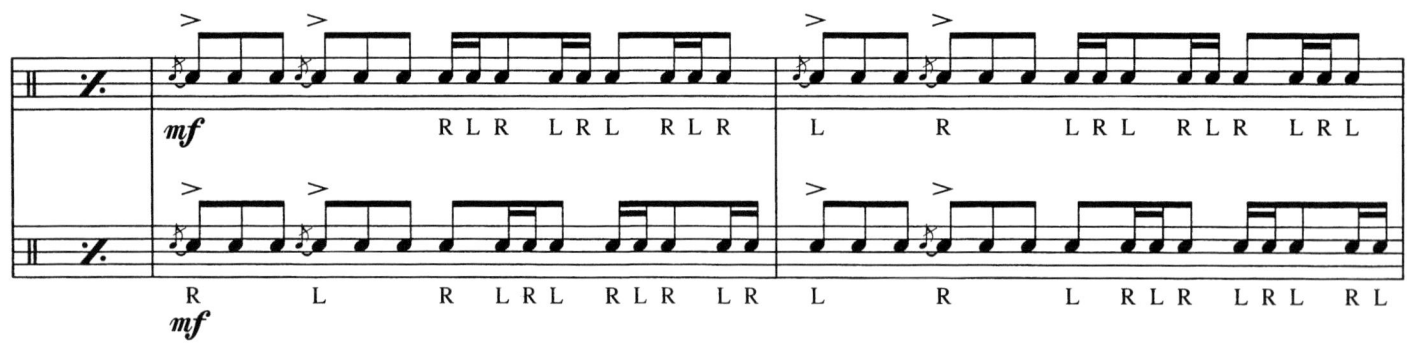
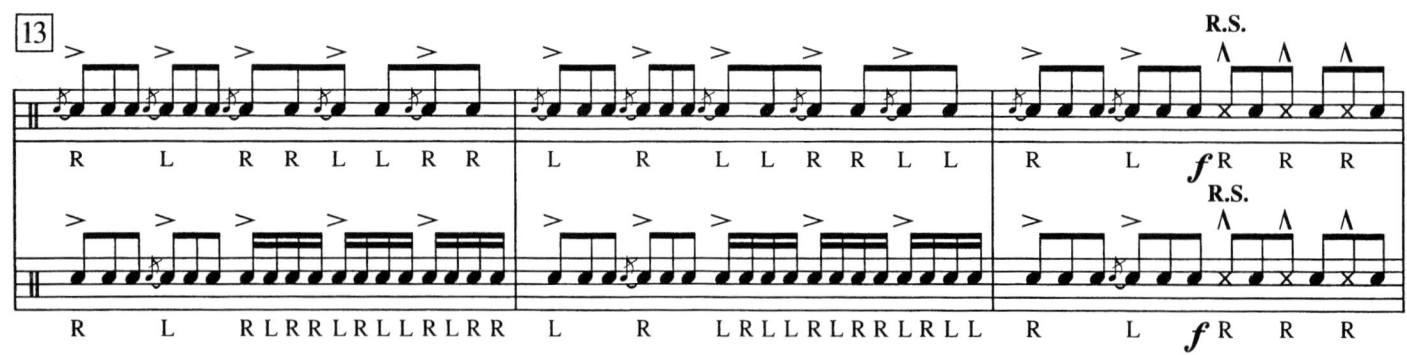

Copyright © MCMXCV by Alfred Publishing Co., Inc.
All rights reserved.   Printed in USA.

Legend:

R.S. (Rim Shot) — Strike the drum so that the stick strikes the drumhead and rim simultaneously.

R.C. (Rim Click) — The butt end of the left stick strikes the rim while the left palm holds the shoulder of the stick in the center of the drumhead.

D.R.S. (Double Rim Shot) — Both sticks should strike the drum and rim simultaneously.

Chop Builders

Jay Wanamaker

1.

2.
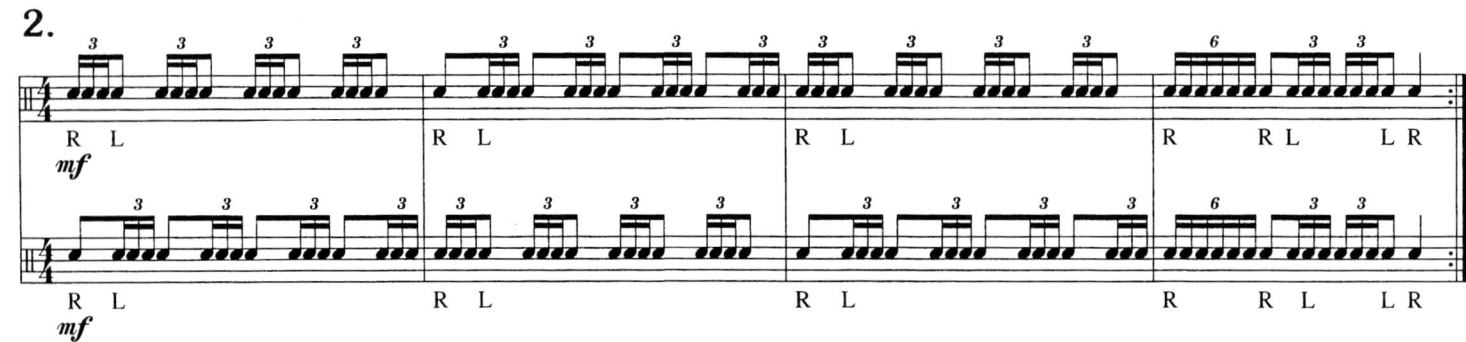

3.

4.
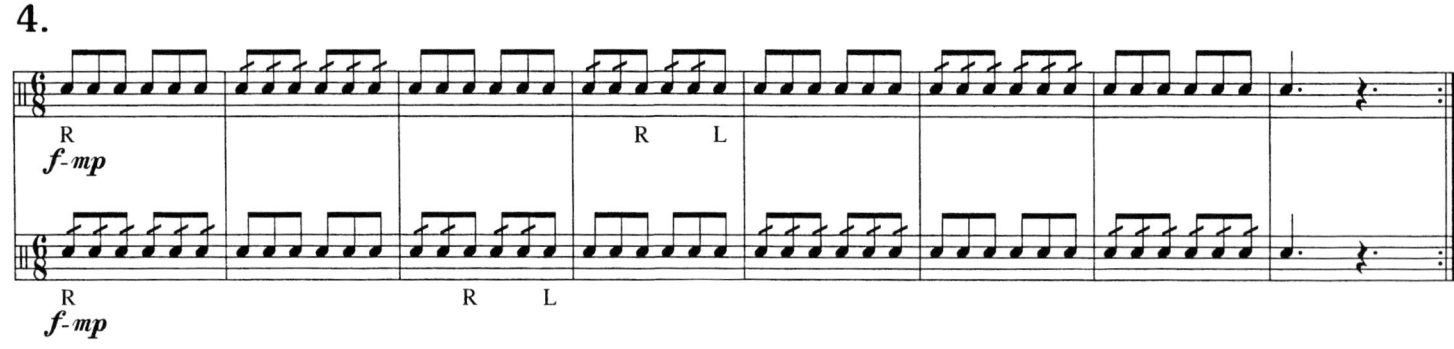

5.
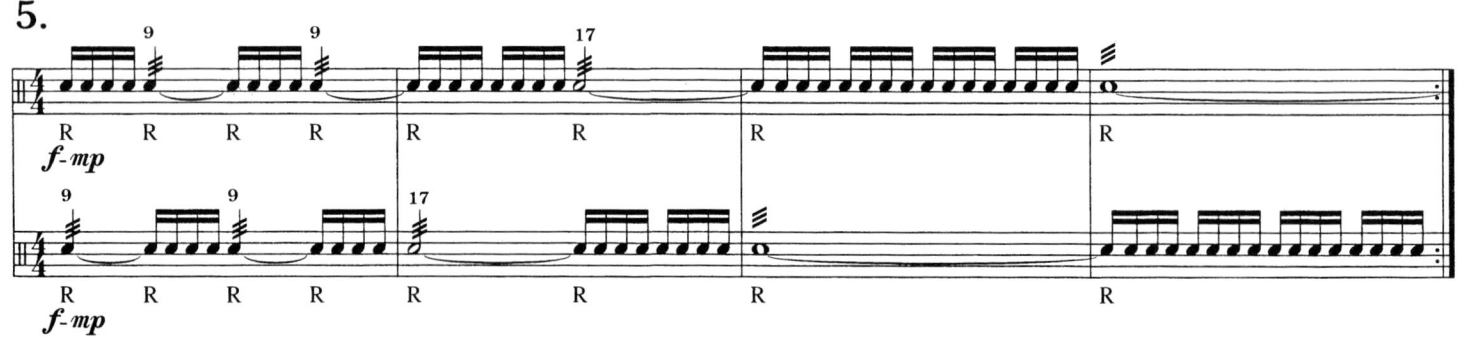

Copyright © MCMXCV by Alfred Publishing Co., Inc.
All rights reserved.   Printed in USA.